Ce

MATH IT!
COUNT IT!

by Nadia Higgins

pogo

Ideas for Parents and Teachers

Pogo Books let children practice reading informational text while introducing them to nonfiction features such as headings, labels, sidebars, maps, and diagrams, as well as a table of contents, glossary, and index.

Carefully leveled text with a strong photo match offers early fluent readers the support they need to succeed.

Before Reading

- "Walk" through the book and point out the various nonfiction features. Ask the student what purpose each feature serves.
- Look at the glossary together. Read and discuss the words.

Read the Book

- Have the child read the book independently.
- Invite him or her to list questions that arise from reading.

After Reading

- Discuss the child's questions. Talk about how he or she might find answers to those questions.
- Prompt the child to think more. Ask: How many ways do you know how to count? Can you count by 2s? 5s? 10s? 100s?

Pogo Books are published by Jump!
5357 Penn Avenue South
Minneapolis, MN 55419
www.jumplibrary.com

Library of Congress Cataloging-in-Publication Data

Names: Higgins, Nadia.
Title: Count it! / by Nadia Higgins.
Description: Minneapolis, MN: Jump!, Inc. [2017]
Series: Math it!
Audience: Age 7-10. | Includes index.
Identifiers: LCCN 2016005386 (print)
LCCN 2016015802 (ebook)
ISBN 9781620314067 (hardcover: alk. paper)
ISBN 9781624964534 (ebook)
Subjects: LCSH: Counting–Juvenile literature.
Classification: LCC QA113.H5224 2017 (print)
LCC QA113 (ebook) | DDC 513.2/11–dc23
LC record available at https://lccn.loc.gov/2016005386

Series Editor: Jenny Fretland VanVoorst
Series Designer: Anna Peterson
Photo Researcher: Anna Peterson

Photo Credits: All photos by Shutterstock except: Getty, 5, 6-7, 14-15b; iStock, 8-9; Thinkstock, 10-11, 16-17 (10, 9, 6, 3), 18.

Printed in the United States of America at Corporate Graphics in North Mankato, Minnesota.

TABLE OF CONTENTS

CHAPTER 1

· ·

WAY TO COUNT!

Imagine a world where nobody used counting.

Every week, your allowance is a *bunch* of money.

At the store, you pick out *enough* cupcakes. So does your mom.

That world does not work well at all!

We need counting. Counting makes amounts **precise** for everybody.

1 2 3 4 5 6 7 8 9 **10**

tens place

ones place

There are many ways to count. Use your fingers and count one by one.

What happens when you get to 9? Move up to 10.

There's just one **digit** to 9. But 10 has two. It has a 1 in the tens **place** and a 0 in the ones place.

Add some friends, and keep counting. 11, 12, 13, 14...

When you get to a 9 in the ones place, move up to the next 10. Now you have 20.

What happens at 99? It is time to add another digit. There are three digits in 100. There is a 1 in the hundreds place, a 0 in the tens place, and a 0 in the ones place.

THINK ABOUT IT!

How many people does it take to get to 100 fingers? How many hands?

hundreds
place

100

ones
place

tens
place

CHAPTER 2

· ·

FAST AND FASTER

Counting one by one is fine for small amounts. But what if you wanted to count more items? You would need a faster way to count. You could **skip count** by 2s.

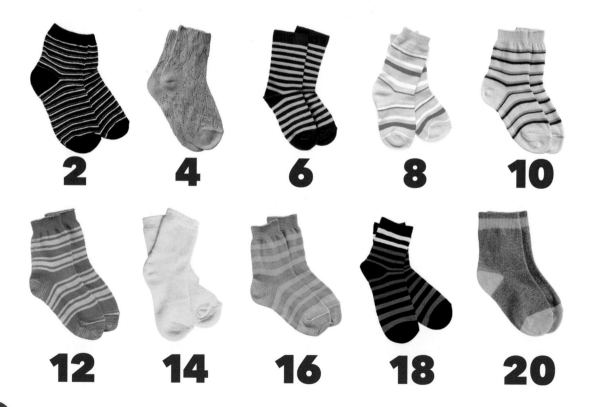

2   4   6   8   10

12   14   16   18   20

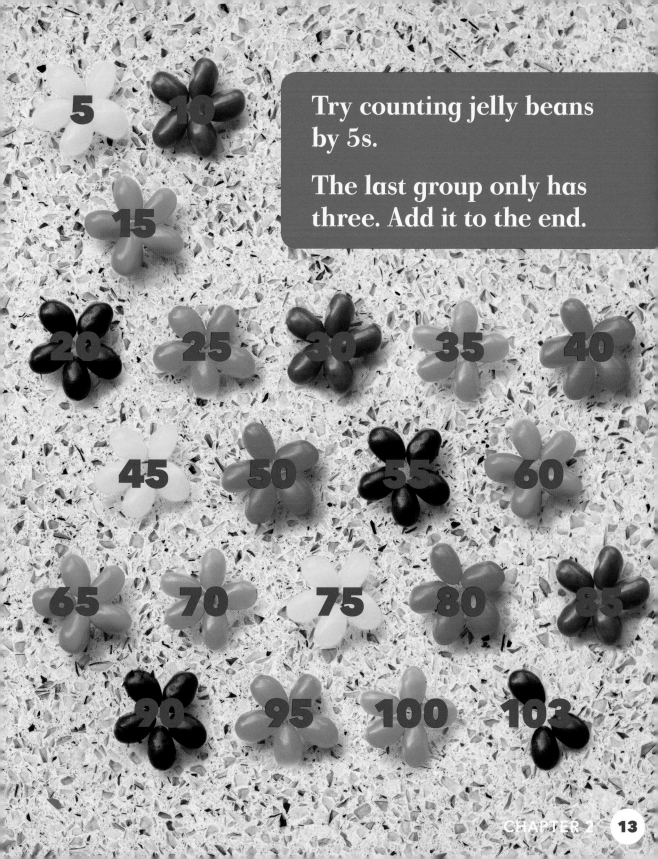

5 **10**

15

20 **25** **30** **35** **40**

45 **50** **55** **60**

65 **70** **75** **80** **85**

90 **95** **100** **103**

Try counting jelly beans by 5s.

The last group only has three. Add it to the end.

In nature, lots of things come in 2s, 5s, or 10s. What is the best way to count the following items?

Count pigeon feet by 2s.

Buttercup petals come in 5s.

Whoops. One flower is missing a petal. Finish counting by 5s. Then add four.

Crab legs come in 10s.

4 6 8 10

15 25 20 30 35 39

20 30 40 50

Some things always come in the same number.

Like what?

10 Bowling pins

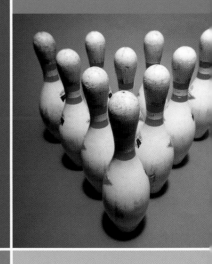

6 Players on a hockey team

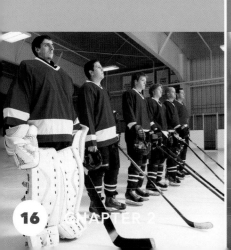

5 Fingers on a hand

4 Seasons

9 Squares in tic-tac-toe

8 Spider legs

7 Continents

3 Sides on a triangle

2 Shoes in a pair

1 You and only you!

CHAPTER 3

HOW HIGH CAN YOU GO?

A **googol** is a number so big, no one ever actually uses it. It has 100 zeroes. Can you count them?

10,000,000,000,000,000,000,000,000,000,000,000,000,000,000,000,000,000,000,000,000,000,000,000,000,000,000,000,000,000,000,000,000,000

10,000,000,000,000,000,
000,000,000,000,000,000,
000,000,000,000,000,000,
000,000,000,000,000,000,
000,000,000,000,000,000,
000,000,000,000,000,000,
00,000,000,000,000 + 1

But you can count even higher than this outrageous number. Just add one. That makes a googol and one!

You can always count higher.
Just keep following the
counting rules.

Ones become tens.
Tens becomes hundreds.
Hundreds becomes thousands.

Thousands become
millions. And on and
on to **billions**, **trillions**,
and more.

Now you know the drill.
So go ahead. Count it!

THINK ABOUT IT!

How long would it take
to count to a million?
Count one number per
second with no breaks.
You would be done
in 11 and a half days.

to the Billions

Ten Milli	Millions	Hundred Thousands	Ten Thousands	Thousands	Hundreds	Tens	Ones
1	8	7,	4	2	9,	5	3	6

ACTIVITIES & TOOLS

GO ON A SCAVENGER COUNT

Look around your home and neighborhood. There must be a million interesting things to count! Can you find answers for these 10 clues? Play with a friend, and make it a race.

1. Trees on the block.
2. Days until your friend's birthday.
3. Stairs to get outside.
4. Bottles in the refrigerator door.
5. Lightbulbs in your bedroom.
6. Things with screens.
7. Words on the first box of food you can find.
8. Steps to walk from your bed to the closest toilet.
9. Red things you can see from a front window.
10. Different sounds you can hear in one minute.

GLOSSARY

billion: A number with nine zeroes.

digit: A 0, 1, 2, 3, 4, 5, 6, 7, 8, or 9 that is part of a number. A digit's value depends on where it is in a number.

googol: A number with 100 zeroes.

million: A number with six zeroes.

place: The value of a digit based on where it is in a number, such as the ones, tens, or hundreds place.

precise: Exact; not at all a guess.

skip count: To count by any number greater than one, but usually by 2s, 5s, and 10s.

trillion: A number with 12 zeroes.

INDEX

TO LEARN MORE

Learning more is as easy as 1, 2, 3.

1) Go to www.factsurfer.com
2) Enter "countit" into the search box.
3) Click the "Surf" button to see a list of websites.

With factsurfer, finding more information is just a click away.